AS YOU LIKE IT,
CHARLIE BROWN

Books by Charles M. Schulz

Weekly Reader Books presents

AS YOU LIKE IT, CHARLIE BROWN

A NEW *PEANUTS* BOOK

By Charles M. Schulz

HOLT, RINEHART AND WINSTON

New York · Chicago · San Francisco

Published simultaneously in Canada by Holt, Rinehart
and Winston of Canada, Limited.

Library of Congress Catalog Card Number: 64-23006

Published, October, 1964

ISBN 0-03-047975-4

Printed in the United States of America

YOU WON'T DO IT, HUH?

NOPE!

I WANT PEOPLE TO HAVE MORE TO SAY ABOUT ME AFTER I'M GONE THAN, "HE WAS A NICE GUY... HE CHASED STICKS!"

AAUGH!

KLUNK

I THINK I'M GETTING MEXICO CITY!

WHAT'S THE MATTER WITH YOU?

MY FINGERS HURT...

MAYBE YOUR FINGERNAILS ARE TOO TIGHT...

I NEVER EVEN KNEW THEY WERE ADJUSTABLE!

THIS HAS BEEN A GOOD DAY!

DO YOU THINK BEETHOVEN WOULD HAVE LIKED ME?

WHY, YES... I THINK SO... I THINK HE WOULD HAVE LIKED YOU VERY MUCH..

A GOOD MANAGER HAS TO BE QUITE TACTFUL SOMETIMES

NEVER TRY TO PLAY JACKS ON A HOT SIDEWALK!

WHAT'S THE DATE TODAY?

TODAY IS THE SIXTEENTH..

I KNEW I HAD THE WRONG THUMB...

ON ODD DAYS I USE MY LEFT THUMB, AND ON EVEN DAYS I USE MY RIGHT THUMB!

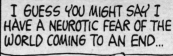

DEAR SNOOPY,
I MISS YOU MORE
THAN I CAN SAY.

I HOPE THEY ARE
TREATING YOU WELL
IN THE HOSPITAL.

WHILE YOU ARE THERE, WHY
DON'T YOU HAVE THEM GIVE
YOU A FLEA BATH?

I SAY THIS, OF COURSE,
AT THE RISK OF BEING
OFFENSIVE. HOPING TO SEE
YOU SOON. YOUR PAL,
CHARLIE BROWN

SUPPERTIME!

!

GOOD GRIEF! I KNEW HE
WAS IN THE HOSPITAL...AND
YET I FIXED HIS SUPPER...

HURRY HOME, SNOOPY..
I'M CRACKING UP!

SNOOPY!

HAPPINESS IS COMING HOME FROM THE HOSPITAL!

THEY TREATED ME VERY WELL IN THE HOSPITAL..

I'LL ALWAYS BE GRATEFUL TO THEM...

I WILL SAY ONE THING, HOWEVER...

IT'S KIND OF NICE TO GET HOME TO YOUR OWN BED AGAIN!

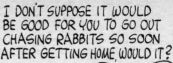

WHAT ARE YOU DOING?

THIS IS A PROJECTOR FOR OBSERVING THE ECLIPSE TOMORROW..

THERE IS NO SAFE METHOD FOR LOOKING DIRECTLY AT AN ECLIPSE, AND IT IS ESPECIALLY DANGEROUS WHEN IT IS A TOTAL ECLIPSE...

THEREFORE, I'VE TAKEN TWO PIECES OF WHITE CARDBOARD, AND PUT A PINHOLE IN ONE.. THIS WILL SERVE TO PROJECT THE IMAGE ONTO THE OTHER BOARD.. SEE?

I'LL BET BEETHOVEN NEVER WOULD HAVE THOUGHT OF THAT!

SO HOW'S THE ECLIPSE?

WE'RE SORT OF STUDYING JOURNALISM IN SCHOOL THIS WEEK...

TODAY OUR TEACHER ASKED US WHAT THE REAL DIFFERENCE IS BETWEEN A MORNING NEWSPAPER AND AN EVENING NEWSPAPER...

I TOLD HER THAT WHEN YOU READ AN EVENING NEWSPAPER, YOU HAVE THE LIGHT ON..

I DIDN'T GET A VERY GOOD GRADE

I THINK MOST OF US TAKE NEWSPAPERS TOO MUCH FOR GRANTED..

WE DON'T REALLY APPRECIATE THE MIRACLE THAT IS THE MODERN DAILY NEWSPAPER...

IT'S DIFFICULT TO PUT INTO WORDS JUST WHY ONE LIKES A NEWSPAPER...

I LIKE A NEWSPAPER BECAUSE YOU DON'T HAVE TO DIAL IT!

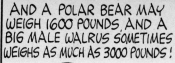

ONCE THERE WAS A TIME WHEN I THOUGHT I COULD GIVE UP THUMB-SUCKING...

NOW I DOUBT IF I EVER COULD..

I'M HOOKED!

SUPPERTIME!

I WAS WRONG...IT ISN'T SUPPERTIME...

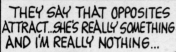

SO WHAT'S THERE TO DO THE **REST** OF THE DAY?

NOBODY LIKES ME...EVERYBODY HATES ME...

WELL, CHARLIE BROWN, IF THE WHOLE WORLD IS EVER AGAINST YOU, I'D LIKE TO HAVE YOU KNOW HOW I'LL FEEL...

WILL YOU BE MY FRIEND?

NO, I'LL BE AGAINST YOU, TOO!

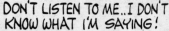

MY SISTER'S HOME!

HERE SNOOPY.. YOU CAN HAVE THE LAST COOKIE..

IF YOU WANT TO SHOW YOUR APPRECIATION, YOU MAY LICK MY HAND

BLEAGH!

DEAR SANTA, HERE IS A LIST OF WHAT I WANT.

HOW DO YOU SUPPOSE SANTA CLAUS CAN AFFORD TO GIVE AWAY ALL THOSE TOYS?

PROMOTION! DON'T KID YOURSELF....EVERYTHING THESE DAYS IS PROMOTION!

I'LL BET IF THE TRUTH WERE BROUGHT OUT, YOU'D FIND THAT HE'S BEING FINANCED BY SOME BIG EASTERN CHAIN!

LUCY SAYS THAT SANTA CLAUS IS CONTROLLED BY SOME BIG EASTERN SYNDICATE...

DON'T BELIEVE HER..THAT'S THE SORT OF STORY THAT GOES AROUND EVERY YEAR AT THIS TIME...

TAKE IT FROM ME..HE'S CLEAN!

BLEAH!

IN FACT, I'LL BET IF ONE OF YOUR REINDEER EVER GOT SICK, SNOOPY WOULD FILL IN FOR HIM, AND HELP PULL YOUR SLED.

DEAR SANTA CLAUS,
I AM WRITING IN BEHALF OF MY DOG, SNOOPY. HE IS A GOOD DOG.

WELL, PERHAPS NOT. BUT HE'S STILL A GOOD DOG IN MANY WAYS.

GOOD GRIEF!

AHEM!

SCHULZ

MONDAY IS BEETHOVEN'S BIRTHDAY!

HAVE A GOOD TIME!

SCHULZ

I GUESS SOMEBODY'S GETTING HUNGRY!

DO YOU KNOW WHY DOGS LIKE PEOPLE?

BECAUSE THEY **NEED** US SO MUCH! WITHOUT PEOPLE DOGS ARE **NOTHING**!

I THOUGHT I'D BETTER LEAVE BEFORE I BEGAN BITING A FEW APPROPRIATE LEGS..

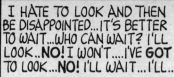

MORE THAN ANYTHING ELSE, THE FEATHER IS RESPONSIBLE FOR BIRDS BEING ABLE TO FLY

FEATHERS ALSO PROTECT THE BIRD'S SENSITIVE SKIN AND ACT AS AN EFFICIENT AIR-CONDITIONER

THE FEATHER IS A MARVEL OF NATURAL ENGINEERING...

SO WHAT WAS **I** BORN WITH? **BEAGLE** HAIR !!

SCHULZ

HAVE YOU EVER HEARD OF A DIATRYMA?

HE WAS A BIRD WHO STOOD SEVEN FEET TALL AND HAD A HEAD AS LARGE AS THAT OF A HORSE! HE HAD A HUGE SHARP BILL AND POWERFUL LEGS WITH WHICH HE COULD RUN DOWN SMALL ANIMALS

HE IS NOW EXTINCT...IN FACT, HE HASN'T BEEN AROUND FOR SIXTY BILLION YEARS...

AND WE DON'T MISS HIM A BIT!

SCHULZ

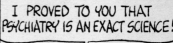

LOOK AT THAT STUPID DOG IN THAT CAR...

HE'S HANGING HIS HEAD OUT THE WINDOW, AND LETTING HIS TONGUE FLAP IN THE BREEZE...

YOU WOULDN'T CATCH **ME** DOING THAT IF I WAS RIDING IN A CAR...

I'D SIT UP STRAIGHT, AND WEAR A SEAT BELT!

WOULDN'T IT BE GREAT IF THAT LITTLE RED-HAIRED GIRL GAVE ME A VALENTINE TOMORROW?

WHAT IF SHE CAME OVER TO ME AND HANDED ME A BIG FANCY VALENTINE WITH LACE ALL AROUND THE EDGE?

WHAT IF SHE SAID TO ME, "DEAREST CHARLIE BROWN, WON'T YOU BE MY VALENTINE? PLEASE? PLEASE? PLEASE?"

I'D BETTER GO IN... I THINK I'M CRACKING UP...

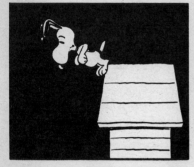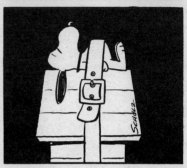

YOU KNOW WHAT'S GOING TO HAPPEN TO YOU?

SOMEDAY YOU'RE GOING TO BE ASKED WHAT YOU'VE DONE DURING YOUR LIFE, AND ALL YOU'LL BE ABLE TO SAY IS, "I WATCHED TV"!

THAT'S WHAT HAPPENED TO GRANDPA...

ALL HE WAS ABLE TO SAY WAS, "I LISTENED TO THE RADIO"

I DON'T **WANT** ANOTHER RABIES SHOT!

WE'RE A COUPLE OF SORE-ARM BUDDIES, DID YOU EVER THINK OF THAT?

YOU HAD A RABIES SHOT, AND I'VE GOT 'LITTLE LEAGUER'S ELBOW'... THAT'S KIND OF FUNNY, ISN'T IT?

I GUESS IT ISN'T...

"RABIES...AN INFECTIOUS VIRUS DISEASE OF THE CENTRAL NERVOUS SYSTEM IN DOGS"

YOU SHOULDN'T BE FUSSING ABOUT GETTING THAT SHOT... YOU SHOULD BE **GRATEFUL**!

WELL, IF YOU'RE **NOT** GRATEFUL, YOU **SHOULD** BE !!

THAT'S BETTER!

YOU BOUGHT SNOOPY A PRESENT?

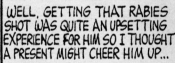

WELL, GETTING THAT RABIES SHOT WAS QUITE AN UPSETTING EXPERIENCE FOR HIM SO I THOUGHT A PRESENT MIGHT CHEER HIM UP...

BESIDES, IT'S SOMETHING HE'S ALWAYS WANTED...

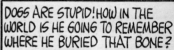

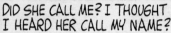